Cambridge **Discovery Education**™

▶ **INTERACTIVE READERS**

Series editor: Bob Hastings

WEIRD WEAPONS

B1

Helen Parker

CAMBRIDGE
UNIVERSITY PRESS

Discovery
EDUCATION

CAMBRIDGE
UNIVERSITY PRESS

University Printing House, Cambridge CB2 8BS, United Kingdom

One Liberty Plaza, 20th Floor, New York, NY 10006, USA

477 Williamstown Road, Port Melbourne, VIC 3207, Australia

4843/24, 2nd Floor, Ansari Road, Daryaganj, Delhi – 110002, India

79 Anson Road, #06–04/06, Singapore 079906

Cambridge University Press is part of the University of Cambridge.

It furthers the University's mission by disseminating knowledge in the pursuit of education, learning and research at the highest international levels of excellence.

www.cambridge.org
Information on this title: www.cambridge.org/9781107652002

© Cambridge University Press 2014

First published 2014
20 19 18 17 16 15 14 13 12 11 10 9 8 7 6 5 4

Printed in Dubai by Oriental Press

A catalogue record for this publication is available from the British Library.

Library of Congress Cataloguing in Publication data
Parker, Helen, 1966-
 Weird weapons / Helen Parker.
    pages cm. -- (Cambridge discovery interactive readers)
  ISBN 978-1-107-65200-2 (pbk. : alk. paper)
1. Weapons--Juvenile literature. 2. English language--Textbooks for foreign speakers.
3. Readers (Elementary) I. Title.

U800.P35 2014
623.4--dc23

                          2013021184

ISBN 978-1-107-65200-2

Additional resources for this publication at www.cambridge.org

Layout services, art direction, book design, and photo research: Q2ABillSMITH GROUP
Editorial services: Hyphen S.A.
Audio production: CityVox, New York
Video production: Q2ABillSMITH GROUP

Contents

Before You Read:
Get Ready!

Humans have used weapons since history began. In this book we look at some of the strangest ideas people have had over the centuries.

Words to Know

Look at the pictures. Then complete the sentences below with the correct words.

atomic bomb

catapult

gunpowder

rocket

sword

target

1 A _____ shoots up into the sky very quickly.

2 A _____ is a long, narrow piece of metal that can cut.

3 A _____ has an arm that can throw things with great power.

4 The _____ is the most powerful weapon in the world.

5 The person or thing that you want to hit is your _____ .

6 _____ was used in bombs to blow things up.

Words to Know

Read the paragraph. Use the highlighted words to complete the definitions below.

The murder of Grigori Rasputin happened in Saint Petersburg, Russia, in 1916. Rasputin had many enemies. Some of them tried to kill him, but they found that this was not so easy to do. At first, the murderers gave him poison – it was not effective. Then they shot him, and a bullet hit him in the back and in the head. It still didn't work. Finally, the killers threw their victim into an icy river where he finally died.

1 _____ : a small piece of metal that comes out of a gun

2 _____ : something that can kill a person or animal if they drink or eat it

3 _____ : bringing the result that you want

4 _____ : a person who has been hurt or killed during a crime

5 _____ : people who are against you in a fight or war

Grigori Rasputin

CHAPTER 1

A Short History of Weapons

HUMANS HAVE ALWAYS LOOKED FOR NEW AND MORE POWERFUL WAYS TO KILL.

Thousands of years ago, the first people made **weapons** to kill animals for food and to attack their human **enemies**. At first, the weapons were very simple and made from stone or wood or both. In cave paintings we can see early people using spears. Boomerangs were also **designed** as hunting weapons.

As humans became more intelligent, they found new and more effective ways to kill. And as people began living in larger groups, they needed more powerful weapons to defend themselves and fight in wars.

These boomerangs were not designed to come back!

Inventors started to use science and technology to invent new weapons. They used metal to make knives and swords, and moving parts to build war machines, like catapults.

And then . . . BANG! The **discovery** of gunpowder in China in the 10th century changed the world of weapons forever.

Suddenly, inventors had something very powerful to use in their **designs**. Gunpowder allowed weapons inventors to make many clever and sometimes unusual ways to kill. Many weapons were designed to kill large numbers of people in wars. Gunpowder could be used to **fire** rockets, cannons,[1] and bombs. Battles became easier to fight at a distance. As in modern wars, **soldiers** did not have to see the people they killed.

Other weapons can murder a victim secretly so that the killer is never caught. But not all weapons are clever or secret. Even normal, everyday things can become dangerous in the hands of a murderer! So watch out!

If you're not already too scared, let's begin our journey through some of history's **weirdest** weapons.

[1] **cannon:** a very large gun

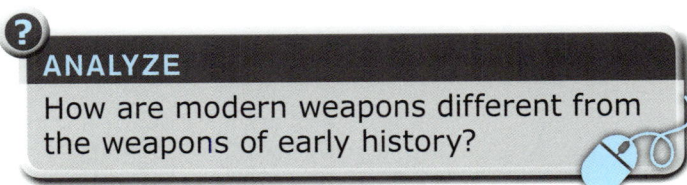

?

ANALYZE
How are modern weapons different from the weapons of early history?

CHAPTER 2

Weapons of War

SOME OF THE STRANGEST WEAPONS WERE INVENTED DURING WARTIME. SOME WORKED, BUT OTHERS WERE TOO CRAZY.

In times of war, army leaders have always spent a lot of time and money on the most effective killing machines. They want weapons that surprise and frighten their enemies. As a result, the weapons inventors through time had to become more and more imaginative.

One of the strangest but most effective war machines was the *trebuchet* (pronounced *treh-boo-shay*). It was used in wars around the Mediterranean[2] from about the 12th century. The trebuchet was a kind of giant catapult.

[2]**Mediterranean:** the sea between southern Europe and northern Africa

How did the trebuchet work? It used a heavy weight to move a long arm very quickly. A sling[3] was tied to the end of the arm. When the weight dropped on the other end, the arm flew up very quickly, and the sling threw

rocks, burning oil, or other dangerous things at the **target**. It was a very powerful machine and could throw a 100-kilogram rock about 300 meters!

The machine was even more effective when it was used to throw the dead bodies of animals and people into enemy castles, towns, and cities. Often the bodies carried serious illnesses. The people inside caught these illnesses and became very sick and died.

It is no surprise that the people of the Middle Ages were terrified of the trebuchet!

[3]**sling:** a piece of material used to hold something

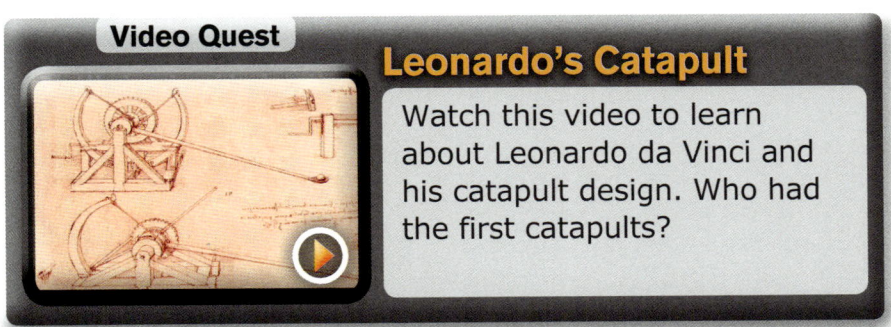

Video Quest

Leonardo's Catapult

Watch this video to learn about Leonardo da Vinci and his catapult design. Who had the first catapults?

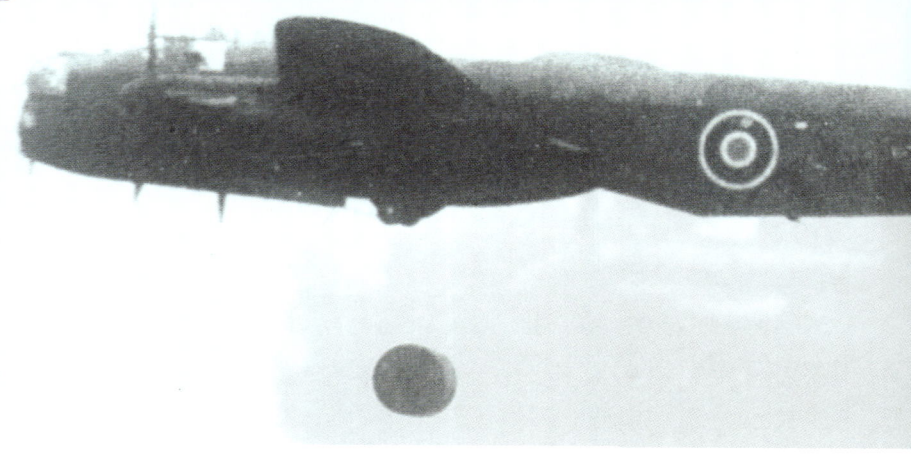

Several centuries later in southern India, the British army was terrified by another strange but effective weapon: the Mughal sword rocket.

At the Battle of Pollilur in 1780, the British soldiers were surprised to see thousands of rockets flying at them. And these rockets had swords tied to them! The British were so frightened of this terrible weapon, they had to surrender.[4]

The Mughal sword rocket was a simple, but clever, idea. First, you take a sword and tie a metal pipe to it. Then you fill the pipe with gunpowder – this makes it a rocket. Next, you light the gunpowder and . . . BOOM! The rocket carries the sword up through the air to attack your enemy.

The sword rocket was a great success, and the British copied the idea themselves in future battles.

....

[4]**surrender:** stop fighting; give up

A bouncing bomb from World War II

Ideas for unusual weapons can often come from simple things. The bouncing[5] bomb is a good example of this. It was used in World War II.

Sir Barnes Wallis, a British engineer, knew that Germany had several important dams.[6] He believed that a giant bomb could destroy these dams, and then water from the lakes would flood many German factories. But how could they hit the dams?

One day, Wallis was throwing stones at a lake, watching the stones bounce along the top of the water, when the idea came to him. At that time, planes did not have the technology to drop bombs on an exact target. But planes could drop bombs near the dams. The bombs would bounce along the top of the water until they crashed into the dam walls.

The bouncing bomb may seem like a crazy idea, but it actually worked! In May 1943, British planes destroyed the Möhne and the Edersee dams. The bouncing bomb helped the British win the war.

[5]**bounce:** go up and down like a basketball
[6]**dam:** a giant wall that stops a river to make a lake

Many other crazy ideas for weapons appeared during World War II. Many of these weapons used animals.

Dog bombs

The Soviets[7] trained dogs to look for food under enemy tanks. Before a battle, they didn't give the dogs any food. The idea was that the hungry dogs – now with bombs tied to them – would run to the tanks. The bombs would then explode. Goodbye, enemies (and dogs)!

Sherman tank used by the United States and its allies during WWII

Pigeon bombs

The Americans trained pigeons to recognize an enemy target. The idea was to put pigeons inside a bomb. The pigeons would be able to look through a small window inside the bomb. When they saw the target, they would peck[8] at the window. This guided the bomb to the target. BOOM! Bye bye, enemies (and pigeons)!

[7]**Soviets:** people from the Soviet Union (1922-1991)
[8]**peck:** when a bird hits something with its mouth

Bat bombs

Bats are very small but strong. They can carry more than their own weight. They also like to sleep in big groups under roofs.

The Americans had the idea to put lots of bats (with small bombs on their backs) inside an empty bomb. Then, they would drop the bomb on Japan. The bats would fly out and go to sleep under Japanese roofs. The little bombs would then explode. So long, enemies (and bats)!

Only one of these ideas was actually used in battle – the dog bombs. But this idea didn't really work. The dogs didn't know the difference between Soviet tanks and enemy tanks. So you can imagine what happened!

The other ideas were never actually used because more effective technologies were on their way, including the atomic bomb – probably the craziest and most powerful weapon in human history.

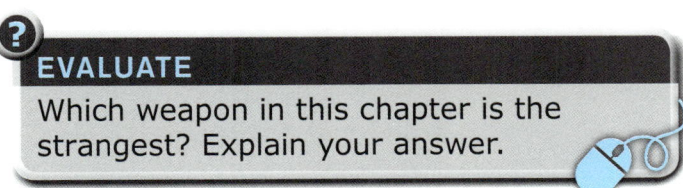

EVALUATE

Which weapon in this chapter is the strangest? Explain your answer.

CHAPTER 3

Murder Weapons

SOME KILLERS WILL ONLY USE THE PERFECT WEAPON. FOR OTHERS ALMOST ANYTHING WILL DO!

Most murderers use "normal" weapons, like guns and knives, to kill their victims. But for some killers, guns and knives are not good enough. They want weapons that are silent and effective. They want weapons that won't leave clues[9] about their identity.

The following story is about a murder with a very unusual but effective weapon. This murder happened during the Cold War, a time when the relationship between the Soviet Union and the West was very difficult. It might seem like a story from a James Bond film, but it is, in fact, completely true.

....

[9] **clue:** something that helps to solve a crime

Georgi Markov was a Bulgarian writer who lived in London. On September 7, 1978, he was waiting for a bus when he felt a pain in his leg. A few moments later, a large man dropped an umbrella. The man said "sorry" then jumped into a taxi.

Markov didn't think too much about what had just happened. He got on the bus and went to his work at the

Georgi Markov

BBC. Three days later, after suffering with a very high temperature, Markov was dead.

The murder weapon was the umbrella. Before he dropped it, the large man had used the umbrella to poison Markov. The umbrella fired a tiny bullet that had poison inside. The poison was ricin, one of the strongest and most dangerous poisons in the world.

No one was ever arrested for Markov's murder, but many people believe that the Bulgarian and Soviet governments organized the killing. Markov often criticized[10] these governments on his BBC radio show. They didn't like Markov at all!

[10] **criticize:** say bad things about someone or something

After the Markov murder, there were other similar killings using umbrellas. For instance, in 2007, an Italian woman died after she was stabbed[11] with an umbrella in a Rome train station. And in 2012, a German man died almost a year after he was stabbed by an umbrella poisoned with mercury. Mercury is a heavy metal that can take a long time to kill.

Another similar and famous murder also happened long after the Cold War had ended. This time the victim was a Russian called Alexander Litvinenko. And this time there was no umbrella, just a strange and powerful poison: polonium-210.

[11] **stab:** push a sharp weapon, like a knife, into someone

On November 1, 2006, Alexander Litvinenko had tea with two men at the Millennium Hotel in London. Like Litvinenko, the two men used to work for the Soviet secret service. Within a few days, Litvinenko became very sick. Three days later, he was in the hospital, but the doctors could do little to help him. In the early morning of November 23, Litvinenko died.

Alexander Litvinenko

Tests on the body showed that Litvinenko had been poisoned by polonium-210. No one has ever been arrested for this murder. Many people believe, however, that one of the Russians at the Millennium Hotel put the poison into Litvinenko's tea. Some people also think that the Russian government was behind the killing. Polonium-210 is very radioactive,[12] and only people close to the government could take it and use it.

Litvinenko believed that the Russian secret service had bombed and killed innocent[13] people. He wrote books criticizing the Russian government. The Russian leaders had a good reason to hate him, but did they really kill him? Only the killers know the true story.

Polonium-210: radioactive and deadly

---

[12]**radioactive:** gives out dangerous energy
[13]**innocent:** did nothing wrong

The murders of Georgi Markov and Alexander Litvinenko were carefully planned, but most murders don't happen that way. Most murders happen after an argument or during a fight. And the murder weapon is often something that the killer finds nearby at the time.

Here are just some of the more unusual things people have used as weapons in the heat of the moment.

A folding couch

In 2008, a Russian woman had an argument with her husband when he refused to get up. She kicked the handle of their folding couch[14] and left the room. She came back three hours later to find her husband had died. The couch had killed him when it folded against the wall.

A fire extinguisher

Len Koenecke was an American baseball player. In 1935, on a small plane flying to Buffalo, he started a fight with the pilot. The plane was moving dangerously from side to side. Something had to be done! The pilot took a fire extinguisher and hit him so hard that Koenecke died immediately.

fire extinguisher

----

[14]**folding couch:** a couch with a seat that can be lifted up to save space in a room

A wooden leg

Sir Arthur Aston, governor[15] of Drogheda, a town in Ireland, had a wooden leg. When an army attacked the town in September 1649, Aston did not surrender. The enemy soldiers thought there were gold coins inside his leg. When they discovered that there was no gold, they hit him with the leg and killed him!

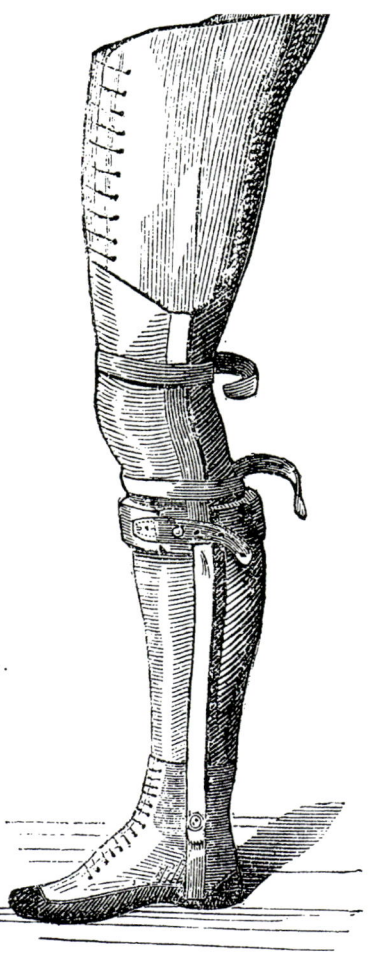

....
[15] **governor:** the head of a government

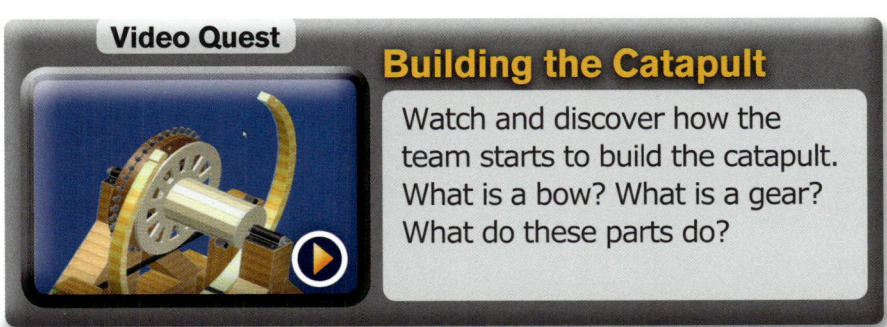

Video Quest

Building the Catapult

Watch and discover how the team starts to build the catapult. What is a bow? What is a gear? What do these parts do?

CHAPTER 4

Killed by Their Own Weapons

"OOPS! I DIDN'T MEAN TO DO THAT!"

Did you know that Marie Curie, who discovered polonium, died after working for many years with radioactive substances?[16]

History is full of examples of people being killed – often accidentally – by their own weapons. Here are two unusual stories of weapons that killed the people who actually designed them.

The Scottish Maiden

You may think of the guillotine as a French invention, but the British began using a similar machine a long time ago. In 1564, a rich and powerful man named James Douglas introduced the Maiden into Scotland.

....

[16] **substance:** a gas, a metal, or other matter

The Maiden was a new way of executing[17] criminals, and a terrifying machine. It was very tall and made of wood. At the top it had a wide blade. This sharp piece of metal dropped down and cut off the head of the victim. It was a quick but unpleasant way to die.

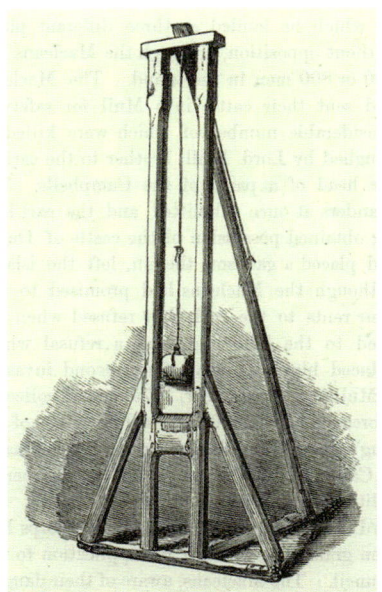

The Scottish "Maiden."—Now in the Edinburgh Antiquarian Museum.[3]

From 1564 until 1710, the Maiden was used to execute more than 150 people. And in 1581 one of those unlucky people was James Douglas himself!

Douglas was executed for his part in the murder of Lord Darnley, the husband of Mary, the queen of Scotland. But many people believe that he was innocent. He was no longer popular with the Scottish leaders, so they got rid of him!

OFF WITH HIS HEAD!

James Douglas, executed with his own machine

[17]**execute:** kill someone as a punishment

Langley Collyer

A room in the Collyer house

The Collyer Brothers

Homer and Langley Collyer lived in a big, old house in New York City, in the early 20th century. As the years passed, the brothers became more and more frightened of the outside world. They put boards over their windows, and Langley designed booby traps[18] to defend the house. Langley had studied engineering and enjoyed inventing and building things.

In 1933, Homer became blind. He now depended completely on Langley to look after him. Langley used to go out at night to find food. People said that he also spent hours going through other people's trash and brought home anything that interested him.

[18]**booby trap:** a hidden weapon that can kill someone when it is touched

On March 21, 1947, someone called the police to tell them that a terrible smell was coming from the Collyers' house – the smell of a dead body. The police broke into the house and found mountains of junk[19] from floor to ceiling. They

began to clear away the junk. There were thousands of newspapers, lots of furniture, a collection of guns, several pianos, and many strange things.

It took a police officer two hours to reach the body of Homer Collyer. Homer had died of hunger, thirst, and a heart attack. But where was his brother, Langley?

The police continued to clear the house looking for Langley Collyer. On April 8, a workman finally found him. Langley had died bringing food to his brother. He had been killed by one of his own booby traps. What a sad way to die!

[19] **junk:** useless things that no one wants

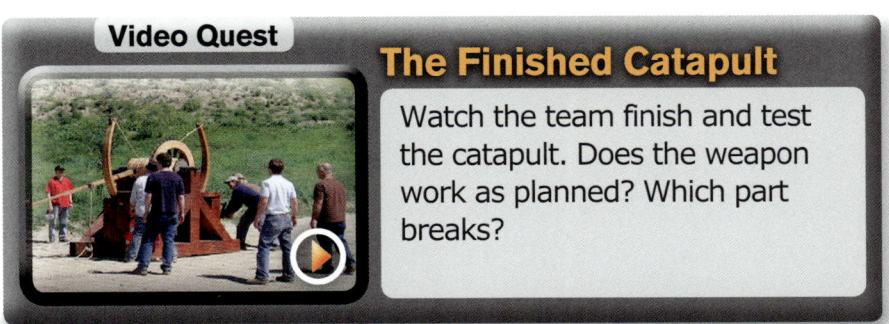

Video Quest

The Finished Catapult

Watch the team finish and test the catapult. Does the weapon work as planned? Which part breaks?

CHAPTER 5

What Do You Think?

WHAT ARE THESE STRANGE WEAPONS? DO YOU THINK THAT THEY WORK?

Before we complete our journey through the world of weird weapons, let's take a look at two very strange inventions. One is a war machine from the 15th century, and the other is a weapon from much more recent times.

Look at the picture above. Who do you think designed it? What does it do? Do you think it actually works?

Leonardo da Vinci designed this giant machine gun around 1480. It has three rows of barrels[20] and used gunpowder to fire bullets at enemy soldiers.

[20] **barrel:** the long pipe of a gun or other weapon

People have built this weapon. It does actually work, and its power is amazing!

Now, look at the photo below. What is it? What are the main parts of the weapon? Do you think it was ever used?

This weapon is a necklace bomb. It has a collar[21] that locks with a key around the neck of the victim. The collar is connected to a box with two pipe bombs inside. There is also a timer inside the box.

On August 28, 2003, in Pennsylvania, USA, Brian Wells robbed a bank wearing a necklace bomb. The police stopped him soon after he left the bank. Wells didn't believe that the bomb was real, but then the timer started to make a noise . . . BEEP, BEEP, BEEP . . . BOOM! The bomb exploded and killed Wells immediately.

The murder was part of a very strange and complicated[22] crime. Go online to read all about it!

....

[21] **collar:** something that goes around the neck of a person or animal
[22] **complicated:** difficult to understand because of many details

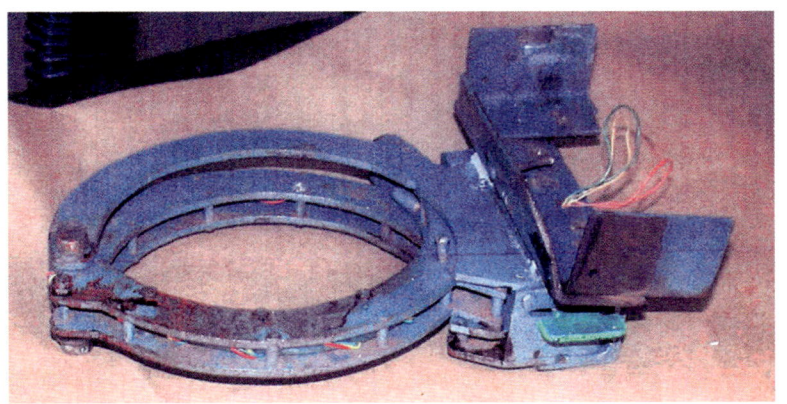

After You Read

Match

Match the weapons on the left with the descriptions on the right.

_____ **1** trebuchet

_____ **2** booby trap

_____ **3** Mughal sword rocket

_____ **4** bouncing bomb

_____ **5** polonium-210

_____ **6** Scottish Maiden

a This flying weapon made the British surrender at Pollilur in India.

b It was used to execute people by cutting off their heads.

c It destroyed two important dams in Germany in 1943.

d It can kill you if you touch it or move it.

e It was used to throw rocks, dead bodies, and other things at the enemy.

f It was used to poison Alexander Litvinenko in London.

True or False?

Choose Ⓐ (True) or Ⓑ (False).

1 The boomerang was designed to be a hunting weapon.
- Ⓐ True
- Ⓑ False

2 Pigeon bombs were a big success in World War II.
- Ⓐ True
- Ⓑ False

3 The Scottish Maiden was an early form of the dog bomb.
- Ⓐ True
- Ⓑ False

4 Leonardo da Vinci designed a machine gun.
- Ⓐ True
- Ⓑ False

Text Completion

Complete the text about gunpowder with the words from the box.

| discovery | effective | enemy | fire | weapons |

The **❶** _____ of gunpowder in 9th century China was an accident, but it became one of the most important substances in the history of **❷** _____ . Gunpowder was used to **❸** _____ rockets, cannons, and early guns. It was also put into bombs, which were used against the **❹** _____ in a war. It was, and still is, a very powerful and **❺** _____ weapon.

Analyze

Think about the weapons in this book. Then fill in the chart.

Which weapon is . . .	Why?
the cleverest?	
the most dangerous?	
the most effective?	
the scariest?	
the most stupid?	

? **EVALUATE**

You are going to make a three-part TV show about weird weapons.

Decide which three weapons from this book you are going to use on the show.

How will you present them? What are the most interesting things about these weapons?

Answer Key

Words to Know, page 4
1 rocket **2** sword **3** catapult **4** atomic bomb
5 target **6** Gunpowder

Words to Know, page 5
1 bullet **2** poison **3** effective **4** victim **5** enemies

Analyze, page 7
Answers will vary.

Video Quest, page 9
The ancient Greeks and Romans had the first catapults.

Evaluate, page 13
Answers will vary.

Video Quest, page 19
The gear drives the drum, which pulls the bow inward.
The bow holds the power to move the throwing arm.

Video Quest, page 23
Yes, the weapon did work. The first throwing arm broke.

Match, page 26
1 e **2** d **3** a **4** c **5** f **6** b

True or False?, page 26
1 A **2** B **3** B **4** A

Text Completion, page 27
1 discovery **2** weapons **3** fire **4** enemy **5** effective

Analyze, page 27
Answers will vary.

Evaluate, page 27
Answers will vary.